"When in Rome..."

Living and Working in a Foreign Country
Personal and Professional Management

by Beverly D. Roman

 BR Anchor Publishing, Bethlehem, Pennsylvania

This publication is designed to provide accurate and authoritative information in regard to the subject matter covered. In publishing this book, neither the author nor the publisher is engaged in rendering legal, accounting or other professional service. If legal advice or other expert assistance is required, the services of a competent professional should be sought.

Printed in the United States of America
Copyright ©1993 BR Anchor Publishing
P.O. Box 176, Hellertown, PA 18055-0176
ISBN 0-9627470-5-X
Library of Congress Catalog Card Number 93-90795
Edited by Cathleen A. Lawson
Illustrated by Michael J. Cadieux

Other books from BR Anchor Publishing
Moving Minus Mishaps, by Beverly D. Roman
    First printing 1991
    Second printing 1992, revised and updated
Leah Anderson's Allentown... The Coloring Book,
    by Leah Anderson, 1991
The Graduate's Handbook, by Beverly D. Roman,
    1992

ACKNOWLEDGEMENTS

Thank you to all the many expatriates who contributed their personal knowledge to the material in this book. These included Americans who lived in Europe and Asia, as well as friends and colleagues from other countries who are living and working in America. Thank you to Aimee Roman, Jonathan Yanover, Paula Brisco, Andy Cummins, and Arny Kaplan, for their comments and suggestions.

Last, but by no means least, I would like to thank Anthony Jenkins, VP, General Manager, Atlas Van Lines International for his invaluable assistance.

Meet the Author

Beverly Roman is a free-lance writer and a small press publisher who specializes in positive relocation products, advice and services. She established BR Anchor Publishing in 1990 and produced her first book, *Moving Minus Mishaps*. Now a revised and updated second edition, 10,000 copies of this book are in print and selling in major bookstores from coast to coast. Beverly wrote *The Graduate's Handbook* for young professionals who have "high aspirations and limited funds" in December 1992. August 1993 saw the debut of *Relocation... 2000*, the company's quarterly newsletter and *"When in Rome..."* marks the fifth book produced by BR Anchor Publishing in less than three years.

The success of *Moving Minus Mishaps*, which is also selling in Europe, and international seminars have established Mrs. Roman as a relocation authority. In demand nationally and abroad, she gives presentations on positive relocation and appears on talk shows, such as ABC TV's "Home Show" and Discovery Channel's "Home Matters."

Beverly and her husband Stan have relocated 16 times in the United States and abroad. They have three grown children who have moved even *more* often. Aimee L. Roman, M.A., Counseling and Psychology resides in Boston, MA, Richard M. Roman, M.D., married to Clara I. Restrepo, M.D., lives in Durham, NC and Christopher D. Roman, M.A. Physiology is a medical student at Georgetown University, Washington, DC.

*This book is dedicated to
our son Christopher
who met the challenge—and triumphed.*

Preface

There has been much written about the trials and tribulations (not to mention, tremendous expense) of international relocation. However, many international relocations are still failing *and* attrition following repatriation still exists.

This book was extremely challenging to write because no one *really* wants to hear the bad news. Neither the corporate personnel nor the employee who is contemplating international relocation.

I did not want to make the decision to *tell it like it is* solely on my own, so I interviewed many people who have "lived the overseas experience." Their overwhelming response was that I should outline for those who are involved—exactly what to expect. As I say in Chapter 4, it is always the unplanned and surprise circumstances that throw us for a loop more than the difficulties we anticipate.

Having experienced 16 moves, domestically and internationally, I firmly believe the level of overall success a family can achieve is directly proportionate to the amount of evaluation, assessment and preparation they receive prior to relocating. Living and working abroad should be all it is meant to be—a unique personal and professional experience. This book is designed to help you achieve these goals. I wish you all the best.

Meet
the
Illustrator

Michael J. Cadieux's lively illustrations are based on his experiences as both an "Air Force brat" who moved with his father many times and continued this tradition on his own throughout the state of Florida. Michael is now settled in Fort Lauderdale where he is an electronic design artist for First Marketing Company.

Moving Minus Mishaps contained Michael's first published cartoon illustrations and opened the way to three other published works and various cartooning projects. His design work for groundbreaking publications gained this graduate of the University of Florida recognition early in his career including a national award for the 1991 annual report for the Broward Economic Development Council. He now spends a great deal of this time on a Macintosh Quadra opening new realms of possibilities for the future of his illustrations and their applications.

CONTENTS

"When in Rome..."

1

"...Do As the Romans Do"

Living and Working in a
Foreign Country: An Overview

I created *"When in Rome..."* to help people who are considering an international relocation prepare for this exciting yet daunting experience. Living and working outside of the United States challenges employees and their families in ways that Americans can never imagine until they actually do it. In the U.S., we are simply not exposed to the diverse cultures a family experiences overseas, nor the work ethics that employees must adapt to and work within. And when in Rome, Paris, Hong Kong, Tokyo, Monterey or Singapore, you must do business "as they do" to achieve immediate and long-term success.

International relocation is so much more complex than moving within and around your own country, which is hard enough. Therefore, I have devoted *"When in Rome..."* to aspects significant to this endeavor. This handbook will outline the "three keys to success:" evaluation of personal and professional details, assessment of family personality traits and preparation to move abroad. Evaluation

13

requires taking stock of what is important to you and your family. You need to decide whether the move and the job opportunity are worth leaving all that is familiar and comfortable to you. Assessment will aid your family in examining your personal adaptability; and preparation will adequately prepare you and your family for a relocation to a new country. Just as important, this book provides tips for a smooth return to your home country.

Working in a foreign country is an opportunity that adds valuable dimensions to your career. In the next decade, cultivating business overseas will be a vital part of day-to-day transactions. Much of this will have to take place away from the home office. The corporate world will see increased global markets; thus, individual companies will have increased foreign assignments. Obviously, whenever a move of this type fails, there is much more at stake for the corporations—and the employees. Failed international relocations have a significant negative impact for everyone. Much more is lost than dollars.

In order to assure yourself that you will be making a positive and successful move, there are many individual questions to face and answer sincerely and fully. One very important consideration of an international relocation is whether you have a working spouse. If so, you are among the 70 percent of married couples in America who do. Of the couples considering an international move, 41 percent have dual-career marriages. Relocation for these individuals is more than a major undertaking, it can also mean the loss of part of their livelihood.

I have designed the information in this book to be beneficial to both the employer and employee. It supplements my primary relocation book, *Moving Minus Mishaps*, which contains 15 checklists and numerous professional resources.

My goal with these two books is to help you to have a win/win situation as you tackle the challenges of international business.

Although overseas relocations are extremely challenging and complex, they can also provide a unique personal and professional opportunity. I believe our four-year assignment in England was one of the most wonderful experiences my family has ever had. Even though we spoke the same language (not true, incidentally), it was still challenging and required a lot of adjustment, personally and professionally. At the end of the day, I would not trade it for anything. The people we met and the places we visited are a treasure trove of memories. I do believe, though, that the three keys to success will prepare you to decide whether to move overseas based upon everything that is important to you and your family.

If you make the decision to relocate abroad for all the *right* reasons, you will not only survive, but excel.

In which country should you never congratulate anyone ahead of an important event such as birthday or wedding because it is considered bad luck?

Note from the author.

We all know that customs and manners vary throughout the world. What is sometimes difficult to understand is how easily people can be offended by a saying, gesture or body language that is considered routine in another country.

To test your knowledge of international customs and manners, see how many of the questions you are able to answer correctly. Quiz questions are at the end of every chapter and the answers are in the back of the book.

2

Evaluation:
The First Step to Success

Before you consider an international move, you and your spouse need to carefully and critically consider what your life will be like in another country. To accomplish this objective you need a substantial amount of information about the specific country you are assessing. Include in your evaluation the social life, customs, education, work standards, housing (size and conveniences), country conditions, and *especially* the security. Think about the effect an overseas transition will have on your family, at home, at school and at work, *at this point* in your lives. Examine your personal and professional reasons for taking an assignment overseas.

The following considerations will help you come to a realistic conclusion about whether you should relocate and why. No matter what country you are considering relocating to, you can obtain information by calling the Overseas Citizen Services listed in Overseas Information Services in Resources and Suggested Reading (referred to after this entry as "Resources"). Also in the Overseas section is *Background Notes* from the Superindent of Doc-

indent of Documents for over 170 countries and references for Japanese literature. Details to order a catalog from Intercultural Press (for various countries) are in the Intercultural Training Section.

Dual-Career Issues

If yours is a two-career family, understand the ramifications of the transfer and how these will affect both your (the candidate's) and your spouse's career plans. Be sure both of your employers are aware of your dual-career status and have a clear understanding of available assistance. Will your spouse be able to work while abroad? If so, examine both overseas positions, as well as the positions to which you will return after the assignment. Evaluate the opportunity, the job description, the political climate of the country, your personal finances and career options. One very important consideration is the candidate's assignment. Is it in an area that requires your business expertise? Will it allow you to grow professionally? If you choose to decline the assignment, what are your alternatives? Don't leave any gray areas in your career planning. See Chapter 8, Dual-Career Issues and Chapter 12, Cultivating Overseas Business.

Children and Schools

The ages of your children will also affect your decision. An initial overseas relocation can lead to additional relocations in other countries. Inquire about this possibility and about what countries could be involved before making a decision. Is your acceptance of the current overseas offer contingent upon further international relocations? Preschoolers, middle school or high school students all require their own evaluation. This evaluation should include the child's level of classroom performance, school activities and other accomplishments in order to choose a school which provides programs to challenge them, yet not require unnecessary struggle. Each child, like each adult, will react differently to a foreign assignment. Children who find companionship and become involved in activities they enjoy will adapt quickly to a new environment. Take into consideration their personality traits and attitudes, a learning disability or any other special requirements as you continue to the assessment phase. Think about all of your children's needs and whether these will be met in another country. Students must be able to successfully matriculate overseas and again on return to the States.

Finances

Include in your evaluation the financial and tax compensation packages your company will provide. How will the income taxes and laws (corporate and personal liability) affect you? Inquire about and evaluate your options for selling or renting your present home. Weigh your personal pros and cons of selling a residence that has been home to your family for a long time. What kind of assistance does your company offer for all facets of housing arrangements, including overseas relocation assistance? Companies who routinely send employees abroad can outline these details, while you will need to fully question and receive thorough answers from those who do not have a program in place.

Medical Concerns

If anyone in your family has a medical problem, discuss the proposed move with your physician. Medications and treatments vary in other countries, so you want to be sure that whatever you require will be available. If you have family members who will remain in your home country, consider whether you need to make provisions, emergency or otherwise, for them. *M3*

And... Finally

Before you proceed to assessment, be sure you spend adequate time evaluating all of these points, as well as adding those that are relevant and significant to your family. If you accept an international relocation but are not adequately prepared, you could face some serious problems. Some expatriates and their families who have not effectively evaluated, nor adequately prepared for their international relocation have experienced alcoholism, depression, boredom and marital difficulties.

No one can weigh the pros and cons of relocation for your family better than you can! This is a decision not to be made in haste, especially if you have school-age children, a two-career marriage and obligations in the States for which you are personally responsible.

In which country should you never propose a toast until a formal toast has been proposed to the queen?

3

Assessment: the Real Criteria

The evaluation process should have helped you determine whether there are any deterring factors that would inhibit an international relocation. The assessment phase will compare your personality traits and attitudes to those of people who have successfully adjusted to foreign cultures. Assessment and selection companies have developed a standard list of characteristics which have been common among all candidates who have adapted well to another culture. Managing cultural changes is mostly a question of *attitude* followed by ample ability and job expertise. Studies show over and over that about 80 percent of success is the talent to effectively lead others and about 20 percent is technical skill.

My area of relocation expertise does not extend to professional assessment. There are companies referenced under Assessment Services in Resources that are far more capable in this endeavor. However, the following questions will get you started. Answer them as honestly and realistically as possible. Afterward, if you have serious doubts about the assignment (and before committing to the move), now is the time to question the offer. I cannot stress the importance of this assessment enough.

There are really no right or wrong answers; however, your responses will make you more insightful about your degree of adaptability. That is really the key issue in overseas assignments: adaptability and willingness to accept the attitudes and methods of others while living and working in another country.

Family Adaptability: Significant Questions

1. Respond to:
   - Do you feel uncomfortable in new and unfamiliar situations?
   - Do you believe you make friends easily?
   - Do you consider yourself adventuresome?
   - Do you believe you take yourself too seriously?
   - Can you laugh at yourself?
   - Have you ever had an experience where you had to adapt to a different standard of living? If so, how did you adjust to the situation?
   - Can you get used to a new situation easily?
   - When greeting people from other countries, do you find yourself thinking that American methods are the best way?
   - When complications and challenges arise, are you still courteous and polite?
   - Have you had any experience conducting business with overseas corporations?
   - Do you believe you are tolerant of others? *Especially* of people from different cultures and ethnic backgrounds?
   - Do you believe you are quick to make a judgement about others?

2. Answer yes or no to the following:
- Do you consider your spouse to be your best friend?
- Will your spouse be able to work overseas?
- Can your family survive on one paycheck?
- Will your spouse relocate if being able to work is not an option?
- Will you both be content if one of you has to commute?
- Will your family be able to continue favorite sports and activities?
- Do you fully understand the overseas assignment?
- Are you committed to making the assignment a success? How committed?

3. Answer and evaluate these two concerns.
- How will your children feel leaving school or sports activities?

  If a student enjoys certain activities or sports which are not available abroad, perhaps others

23

of equal interest may lie ahead. If not, then you need to decide just how important these activities are to the child.

- Do you have family members who will remain in the States who are dependent on you in any way?

  If so, evaluate how important your presence and assistance is to them and discuss how the overseas transition will affect them.

If your answers to the first series of questions leave you in doubt about your level of adaptability, or if you have a two-career marriage and answered no to two or more questions in the second series, you should look into more thorough assessment methods to reevaluate overseas relocation and your options.

There is no such thing as a crystal ball, and no one can ever know how a move will turn out. *But* if you are fairly certain of what to expect in a foreign country, are well-prepared for daily practicalities and understand its business culture and schools, believe me, your chances of achieving success will increase tremendously.

In which country should you be prepared for a great deal of bargaining when making a purchase?

4

Family Preparation

Of the relocations that fail, especially international relocations, 80 percent result from the family's inability (the spouse's in particular) to adjust. That is why I place so much emphasis on thorough evaluation and careful family assessment. Equally important are the following tips for preparation because they will help you to adjust in the new area. This chapter will prepare you so that when you arrive in the new country, you will function comfortably and effectively at home, work and school with the least amount of "downtime"

Even if you have moved many times, you will find that international moves require additional considerations. The basic practicalities for a smooth move are thoroughly outlined in *Moving Minus Mishaps*, and in it you will find expanded information for some of the points in this book, and many aspects of this chapter. These points are designated by the M3 code. I have not repeated these in *"When in Rome..."*, but provided instead, comprehensive information that a family will need to relocate internationally. The following eight-week countdown outlines specifics for moving abroad.

Eight weeks (at least) before you relocate

1. Obtain all necessary documents, such as passport, visa, and if necessary, a nationality ID. See also General International Information in Resources for references and booklets from Consumer Information Center. Allow six to eight weeks for receipt. *M3*

2. It is very possible you will need another language and intercultural training. If so, *inquire about these NOW!* You should have a working knowledge of the new language before moving into the country. Especially greetings, and simple phrases like please and thank you. Ask your employer for references and see Intercultural Training in Resources.

3. Check with the Relocation Department at work to **be sure** that your working papers are being processed.

4. Inquire about the necessary documentation that is required to allow for importation of your household goods and personal effects into the country. Although this is a relatively simple procedure in many countries, some (such as Brazil and Mexico) require six to eight weeks for approval from the host government.

5. Purchase a bilingual dictionary, if necessary.

6. Plan at least one trip overseas to:
   - Survey living arrangements and become familiar with the city.
   - Visit the schools and day-care centers. See *M3* for guidelines.
   - Check into baby-sitters. *See* M3 and the Telephone Number Checklist for a nanny association.
   - Contact a real estate agent to assist you. Be sure to request a relocation package. You may also think about consulting a solicitor. *M3* See also Checklist in this book for Househunting Trip Abroad.

7. If you do not already have a VISA or MasterCard, apply for at least one of them because they are readily accepted abroad. Also, apply for a four-digit personal identification number (PIN). With this number, you can use your credit cards in automatic teller machines.

Seven weeks

1. Make a **complete inventory** of your household effects with serial and model numbers. *M3*
2. Now is a good time to plan a garage sale. This is a wonderful method to clean house and avoid moving or storing unwanted items.
3. Determine which appliances you can move overseas. Some appliances will not work adequately nor fit into

the smaller accommodations in overseas homes. Also, a few countries restrict the number of appliances you can move with you. It can be difficult to obtain repairs or parts for U.S. appliances in some countries.

See pages 82-83 to learn more about appliances from Appliances Overseas, Inc. *Mention BR Anchor Publishing* to receive *complimentary* information from Appliances Overseas for your country.

4. Evaluate your furniture to decide what to store and what to move abroad. *M3* See page 30 and House-hunting Checklist.

5. Book airplane travel for your-selves and your pets. Booking should be done early because it is best if your pets can trav-el as near to your travel time as possible (and during the cooler times of the day). The airline may have tourist infor-mation about the country; ask for details. See Checklist in *M3* for Pet Supplies for Inter-national Travel.

Five to six weeks

1. Consider purchasing an International Driving Permit. These documents serve as an excellent form of identification because they are printed in several different languages. They are valid for a one-year period and useful for short stays or to use until you acquire a permit in the country. See General International Information in Resources to order. (Be sure your present drivers license does not expire while you are away.)

2. Obtain insurance for autos and household goods. Set up these services so they are effective upon your arrival in the foreign country. Understand your med-

ical coverage. See Chapter 10, Insurance Coverage and the Checklist on page 77.

3. File address changes with the post office. Discuss mail forwarding and possible mail restrictions in the country with your postmaster. M3

4. Collect more details about the country and its culture. Check with your corporation, public library and travel agencies.

5. Talk with colleagues who have lived in the country. Ask about problems they experienced, suggestions for easiest acclimation and fun activities or sights.

6. Do not overlook security services in the country. Your employer should have information on the country you are considering. See Overseas Information Services for information on The Travelers Advisory System.

7. Update your will and consider obtaining a power of attorney for the time you will be overseas.

We thought you might want to take a break here to answer a Customs and Manners question.

In which country is it considered very bad manners if you have more wine than you can graciously consume?

Three to four weeks

1. Confirm all moving plans and go over storage and packing decisions with the movers.

2. Confirm your insurance coverage with your employer for furniture you wish to store. M3

3. Inquire about opening an overseas bank account.

4. Learn who to contact for medical emergencies. M3

5. Practice your new language and review the information about the country that you collected.

6. Purchase a money pouch (fanny pak) for anyone in

your family who will be traveling on their own. These are safer than carrying a purse or a wallet.

7. Purchase luggage tags for the entire family with your names and address.

8. Arrange for absentee voting.

One to two weeks

1. Learn about the country's governmental, social, medical and other important organizations. Know who and how to contact for assistance.

2. Check with your corporate office for telephone numbers and access codes to call within the foreign country, as well as how to call the U.S.

3. Be sure family members at home have a practical method to contact you while you are abroad. They should also have the home and work numbers of several stateside contacts from your corporation. See Chapter 7, Medical and Emergency Precautions and General International Information in Resources for IAMAT

4. Obtain information about the driving rules, laws and customs regulations in the country. Review these prior to moving to avoid (unknowingly) breaking the law. See Overseas Information Services in Resources.

5. Decide what you will require before your household goods arrive and make arrangements for an air shipment. Consider your clothing, school books, and personal items. The shipment of your goods will take approximately five to six weeks.

6. Request a variety of currency from your bank for the country to which you are moving so you will have ready cash on arrival for transportation or a telephone call. Travelers checks may be available in this cur-

rency as well and these are handy to use until you become financially established.

7. If you are taking a computer, back up all your computer files and check the manual for the procedure to "park the heads."

As you plan your move, critically evaluate the items you plan to take overseas. You probably want to take your own bed (and extra sheets because linen sizes will vary from U.S.), comfy furniture used daily and personal items, such as family pictures and mementos. Use discretion, because you can easily purchase furniture, lamps and appliances plus numerous other household goods abroad through overseas organizations. Many countries have women's organizations who can help you in this endeavor. You can find perfectly good second-hand items that you can sell before you return to the States and everyone will be richer for the bargain: the buyer, seller and your company. See also Checklist in this book for Househunting Trip Abroad.

Careful planning and preparation will minimize confusion tremendously. It is always the unplanned and surprise circumstances that throw us for a loop more than the difficulties we anticipate. While living overseas, I heard many people say: "If only I had known what to expect." Don't let that happen to you! If you have decided to make this move, find out everything you possibly can about the country, culture, working conditions and everything that affects your family—before you move!

Note: U. S. Embassies are located in 144 capital cities of the world. See Overseas Information in Resources.

In which country is it socially acceptable to imbibe in excess after working hours?

31

Managing Your Emotional Baggage
by Roger J. Cadieux, M. D., Associate Professor of Psychiatry
Pennsylvania State University, College of Medicine

Relocating to another country can be an enriching experience resulting in personal and professional growth, as well as closer family ties. On the other hand, the stress involved in relocation can result in social, emotional and physical problems which can defeat the benefits of such a move.

Stress is a fairly predictable response to change of any type. Good things can happen when we mobilize our anxiety and seek solutions to specific problems. Unrecognized or ignored stress can result in physical and emotional illness. The solution to "relocation stress" is to acknowledge its potential and then to implement effective coping mechanisms towards reducing it. Mastering a person's family and job related stress should involve the following:

- Education. Learn as much about the anticipated move as possible. What are the demands of the new job? What are the social and cultural requirements? Who should you contact for continuing physical and emotional care?

- Rapport. Keep the lines of communication open between all interested parties. Knowing what you and your family's reasonable limits are regarding the demands of relocation can help in accepting or demarcating the challenges of the job.

- Taking a Planned Risk. What is it going to take to make this move work? Life is a series of risks. Those who plan for them, rather than approaching them impulsively or at the last minute, minimize their stress while reaping the benefits of positive personal and family emotional growth.

- Remembering the Home Front. What does my family need so they can become the best support system that I have when I arrive at my new position? Make sure that you give equal priority to personal as well as job related demands in planning for your move.

5

Concerns for Children

If you and your spouse are firmly convinced that an international relocation is the right choice for your family, then you can explain the move to your children *with* conviction and enthusiasm. Career moves do not have any meaning to children, so explain why you believe the decision is the right one for your family and how you plan to make the most of this adventure.

This presentation needs to be appropriately timed and carefully explained in a manner that is relevant to each one of your children. Speak openly and often about the move and encourage lots of questions about their concerns.

It is as important to assess your children's ability to adapt to a new culture as it is to assess your's. Have your children answer the questions in Chapter 3, then review as a family. In addition, intercultural training will speed adjustment into a foreign country. High school students, in particular can have a difficult time relocating abroad. Much depends on the students themselves. It is *very important* that they answer these questions realistically and honestly. If you have any concerns, identify them and seek professional advice.

To help young people adapt, learn about the country through books and pictures. For information, check public and university libraries, American Automobile Association (for members), airlines. In addition, major moving companies provide packets with foreign country overviews. These packets include details about the climate, time zones, weather, currency, housing, transportation, just to name a few. Share all of this information with

Isn't he adapting just a bit too quickly?

your children, so they can construct a visual image of their new home. Have children give their address to grandparents and friends to encourage correspondence.

Think about your children's favorite pastimes as well as their activities. Many children are used to CDs, television computer games and walkmans. Consider how you can arrange for continuity of these. See *M3* for details about using a U.S. television on a transformer in another country.

Preschoolers

Preschoolers' worlds and identities revolve around their family and home. Children at this age can feel threatened when they see moving personnel packing their bed, toys and personal belongings. Assign a few manageable chores to these children to keep them occupied and help them feel important to the moving endeavor. Survival boxes are an excellent method to ease young children's fear of mislaying favorite "things." See *M3* for description.

Grade School Children

Grade school-age children have extended their horizons outside of the home and their interests focus more on friends and school. However, they may worry about such details as finding their way home, finding a room in their new school, boarding the right school bus or getting off the bus at the correct stop. Take the time to learn about and address their thoughts and concerns, so you can allay their fears. Even though they may be sad to leave good friends, they're also eager to experience new adventures.

Teenagers

School transitions are *very* challenging for teens. Don't underestimate the effect relocation can have in addition to a change of school. Listen carefully to your teenagers' concerns and take time to address each of these. Their biggest fear is usually acceptance by their peers in the new area. If a teenager is having difficulty making friends in a new school, talk to the school counselor. Some schools have a newcomers club or some means of getting new students involved. The unhappy face sitting across the dinner table from you is rarely seen at school, so teachers may not be aware of problems you are experiencing. Don't hesitate to approach the teacher and discuss your concerns.

College Students and Young Adults

If your college age children will attend school abroad, consult the suggested resources in Chapter 6, Education: Points to Consider to learn where to get information about universities and educational programs. The atmosphere, instructors and schedule in overseas schools will contrast from those in the States. Ensure that the courses and studies will correlate with programs in the U.S., so that your student can easily transfer to an American university, further their degree and be competitive in the U.S. market. Here again, you and your student should evaluate all options. Studying abroad can be a unique and maturing experience, educationally and socially.

If your "grown-up" children remain in the United States, remember that they *still* need the TLC and moral support of their parents (although they may not often admit it). A great ocean and varying time zones lie between you and your "at home" family. Everyone feels these distances. An answering machine is standard in most homes today, but when part of the family is living overseas, it becomes a must. Some friends of mine use a fax machine to communicate with their children, because of a 16-hour time difference. Research the cost and practicality of this method to see if this would work for you.

When you or your adult children are excited about a special event in your lives, the moment may be lost if you cannot share it with each other. You can close long distance gaps a bit by telephoning, leaving a message on an answering machine or relaying your thoughts and activities via a fax machine.

Be sure young adults have the State Department's Citizens Emergency Center number, (202) 647-5225. See Chapter 7 Medical and Emergency Precautions for more information.

If you have colleagues abroad who have children, introduce them before school begins. Children who have already moved abroad are aware of the challenges and are anxious to help newcomers become acquainted. One such challenge includes mastering the local lingo. So even if you move to an English speaking country, such as New Zealand, England, Ireland, Scotland, Canada or Australia, you will hear different terminology because America has added its own slang to the English language.

No two children are alike. Some will slip into a new environment and culture without so much as a casual glance back at their former lifestyle. Others can be most profoundly affected by a relocation to a new environment with new friends. Parents can usually tell very quickly if their children are experiencing problems.

Watch for changes in daily attitudes, habits, attire and moods. Signs of adjustment problems that children can experience and suggestions to help them adapt are fully outlined in *M3*. With your care and support, your children can not only survive but enjoy themselves—and later consider the experience a growing one.

Note: If you would like information about nannies in other countries, see The Telephone Numbers Checklist and *M3* for The International Nanny Association.

In which country should you never tease
or kid someone playfully because it could be
misinterpreted and considered offensive?

6

Education: Points to Consider

Because education varies from country to country (even region to region), it is impossible to discuss all aspects of international education. Rather, I have provided specific points for you to review and have listed references to assist your search for optimal schooling.

International moves require careful examination of the country's and locality's academic programs. Correlate courses for matriculation abroad and for return to your home country. Visit schools or child care centers and chat with the teachers or supervisors *before* your children begin attending. This visit and communication will assist you in forming an opinion of the school environment, values and capabilities and the personalities and skills of teachers.

Have "dry runs" from the new home and school bus stop, especially for very young children. Children can get distracted or lose their way, so stress the importance of using the same route every day and coming straight home. This exercise will enable you to trace their path if they do not arrive home when you expect them.

Criteria to select a school and more information on

international schools, as well as descriptions of curricula and services for the following international schools are outlined in *M3*.

- The Association of Christian Schools International
- Private Independent Schools
- International Schools Services

See the International School section of Resources for more details about the following two publications which contain information about university and professional schools.

1 *International Schools Services Directory*. An annual directory that has comprehensive information on international and American schools around the world as well as jobs and internships. See Resources for accessibility.

2 *The World of Learning*, Europa Publications. This directory contains complete details for over 26,000 universities, colleges, schools of art and music, research institutes, libraries, art galleries and others. Also included is an extensive listing of over 400 major international organizations concerned with education worldwide and a 100 page index.

Check your children's transcripts before leaving the States to ensure they are complete. Each school system has a different requirement for the number of transcripts they require; some may need numerous copies. Understand the school requirements and academic programs of study in your child's new school and share this information with present teachers and counselors. A letter to outline current special programs in which your children are involved may be helpful to the administration at the new school. If you think this would benefit your children, ask their present teachers to write and forward specifics.

Adjusting to a new school and country is difficult enough; struggling with social mores will certainly compound the situation. If one of your students cannot comprehend a subject's material, encourage them to speak to their new teachers ASAP. Determine ways to best maintain education continuity and stay close to your children until you believe they are acting and reacting much the same as in their former environment.

In which country should you never give someone a slap on the back because it would be considered rude?

"WHEN IN ROME ..."

7

Medical and Emergency Precautions

Moving, especially internationally, puts added stress on people's lives. As a result, they are more likely to experience an accident or contract a disease or illness. I speak from experience when I say **do not travel to any foreign country until you know where to obtain emergency care and contacts**.

Prior to departure, you and your family should have a thorough medical, dental and, if appropriate, eye examination. To assure continuity of medical care, take along that important list of your family's medications, treatment and medical tests and the results. Records about illnesses, surgery and broken bones are very important to the care and well-being of your family. Personally carry your family's complete list of medications and *don't* underestimate the possibility of drug interaction. Any medications that you take with you should be in their own well-marked container. Everyone traveling or moving abroad needs to know how to obtain care *before* their arrival in the country. See the checklist for Family Medical in this book.

You will find that the laws governing drugs can vary considerably in other countries. If someone in your family is taking a prescription drug, I would advise you to have a discussion with your doctor and thoroughly understand all your medications, side effects and the rules that govern its usage. Some drugs sold over-the-counter or by prescription in America may be illegal in other countries, and vice versa. In some foreign countries, the penalties for illegal possession and/or usage of drugs can be very harsh.

After you arrive in the new country: visit the local medical facility ASAP. As I mentioned earlier, it is important to have medical care before you leave the U.S.; however, I still advise you to visit the medical facility to become acquainted and learn about procedures and routines for medical (especially emergency) care.

See M3 for *complete* details about international medication and guidelines for physicians plus more information about IAMAT. See also General International Information in Resources to order a booklet from IAMAT (International Association for Medical Assistance for Travelers). If your family needs to reach you because of an emergency at home or because they are worried about your welfare, they can call the State Department's **Citizens Emergency Center at (202) 647-5225**. The Department will relay the message to consular officers in the country in which you are living or traveling. The consular officers will then attempt to locate you, pass on urgent messages and, consistent with the Privacy Act, report back to your family.

Even if you and your family are blessed with good health and medical concerns are the furthest thing from your mind, heed these suggestions. I could tell you more war stories about moving and accidents than we have space for in this book. As I said in the beginning of this section, moving puts increased strain and stress on people and it never fails that the time when you least expect it, an accident can (and often does) happen. Moving overseas will take you a long way from 911.

Note: Immunizations must be up-to-date. Many countries, such as Algeria, Africa and Southeast Asia, to name a few, require vaccines. Call the Centers for Disease Control for updated immunization requirements in specific countries. Telephone (404) 332-4559.

In which country is it proper to address surgeons and dentists as "Mister," instead of "Doctor?"

"WHEN IN ROME ..."

8

Dual-Career Issues

Before Accepting the Overseas Position

If you are considering an overseas assignment with a dual-career family, you definitely have some critical issues to consider. When you completed the evaluation section of this book you considered *everything* that is happening in your life right now. If you decided that the international opportunity will be a pivotal point in your (the candidate's) career, you and your spouse must now look at the options available for a working spouse. These options include:

- Your spouse continues to work for his/her present employer, but in another capacity abroad.
- Your spouse remains in his/her position in the U.S.
- Your spouse will relinquish his/her job and attempt to secure a new position abroad.
- Your spouse will redefine work through volunteering or taking courses to further a career.

If your spouse wants to remain with the same company he/she needs to approach the employer to present ideas for change. Some suggestions include: research, writing or utilizing telecommunications. Perhaps the international relocation can somehow benefit the spouse's company, as well.

If your spouse chooses to stay in the States, remember that working worlds apart can put tremendous strain on marriages and families. You will need to plan frequent "reunions" and communicate often.

The last two options will mean setting aside career goals, as well as relinquishing contacts, networks and benefits. Financial compensation for the overseas assignment may partially make up the loss of one salary; however, giving up a job means more to the person involved than forfeiting an income.

If your spouse wants to work overseas, but must resign from his/her current position, he/she will need to research the possibility of a work visa *before* you move into the country and update his/her résumé. In this event,

you, as the candidate, should inform your employer of the circumstances and request assistance. I am not suggesting a salary supplement but practical guidance from Human Resources or a professional career strategist.

Lastly, if your spouse has chosen to redefine work, here are alternatives that have proven successful:

- Taking courses to further a career.
- Doing personal or company research.
- Taking a leave of absence and/or contributing to charity work. Volunteering adds a quality nonsalaried occupation to current professional accomplishments. For instance, being instrumental in restructuring a

charitable organization involves many of the skills used in positions that draw paychecks.

Potential Problems

Expatriates have experienced the following points as problems in some countries *more than* others. Learn about the country you are considering to see how to manage these situations.

- Obtaining a work permit abroad. (After you leave America, this can be very difficult for a spouse who has not been relocated at the request of his/her employer.)
- Foreign biases against working women.
- Obtaining a job. (It may be extremely difficult to find any kind of meaningful employment, charity work or fulfilling endeavors in some countries.).
- Visas—forms and required documents.
- Immigration questions—offices and procedures.
- Dangerous living conditions.

While Abroad

Your spouse should:
- Be sure to keep a log of activities to assist job-seeking efforts when you return to the States.
- Note any additional skills learned, such as managerial or language and add them to your résumé
- Obtain letters of recommendation, especially from well-known companies with which he/she has worked.

It is important that you both understand *all* of your options and career opportunities. If you decide to move, know how much of a command of another language is required, and understand the country's employment laws and political climate.

49

This work dilemma will not go away. The number of dual-career couples is increasing, both domestically and internationally. Since you are both working for a common goal and sharing financial responsibilities, you need to carefully and critically examine all your options. If you are relocating abroad, dual-career or not, you *must* travel as a team.

See also Chapter 12, Personal Business Strategies and Resources for Overseas Information Services and International Business and American Firms Abroad.

In which country will you insult your hosts
if you leave a dinner party early? These people
love to visit until the wee hours of the morning.

9

Selecting a Moving Company

Most international relocations are corporate transfers; therefore, your company may already have an account with a moving company. However, if you are choosing your own company, I suggest surveying three well-qualified international moving companies. Ask for personal references of satisfied customers and compare their prices, services and policies. Inquire about the type of containers, method of shipment that they use and the effect these will have on your household goods. See also Insurance Coverage. Whatever company you choose, book your moving date as soon as possible and confirm your arrangements as you get close to the packing and departure dates.

Know the procedures and insurance coverage provided by this company and your own corporation. Keep all luggage and personal documents, such as medical records, insurance forms, school records and passports, *separate* from items to be packed. Photocopy all valuable documents. Take the copies with you and put the originals in a safety deposit box in your home country. See Personal Documents Checklist in this book and *M3*.

In addition:
- Request overseas literature.
- Be sure the moving company has excellent dry storage facilities.
- Check the type of padding used. Bubble wrap should not be used directly on wood.
- Find out the company's capabilities to place packed boxes into large wooden crates. By storing numerous boxes in one large crate, the individual boxes will be better protected.
- Know the telephone number of the overseas moving company and put the contact person on your "to do" list for when you arrive in the new country.
- Know the approximate date of your shipment arrival. Carry with you items or clothing that you will need until your household goods arrive.

When you plan your move, book the dates and packing schedule as specifically as possible. After agreeing on the date, the mover must abide by this schedule or notify you of a problem causing a delay. You, or a responsible person, should be at your new residence at the agreed upon time of delivery. Every good move is a cooperative effort between the mover and the family who is moving. Work with your movers, learn their names (and use them often). If you follow the suggestions in M3 to organize your furniture in room plans, you will be surprised how smoothly the whole procedure will proceed.

In which country is it unnecessary to stay in an expensive hotel to create a better image?

10

Insurance Coverage

First and foremost, prepare a household inventory. It is to your advantage to have an accurate, up-to-date account of your household goods. *M3* If *you* do not declare the value of your goods, the moving company will have to estimate the value.

Understand your corporate insurance coverage and then check with your own insurance agent to be sure your goods are comprehensively covered during the move. Many corporate overseas insurance policies will be Replacement Cost policies. These usually cover theft, vandalism, fire and breakage caused by auto collision. However, replacement policies do not cover two common moving problems: breakage caused by packing items yourself and damage caused by shifting of the load.

You may purchase coverage for these breakage problems on a temporary basis from the mover or for permanent coverage from your agent, through a policy called a floater. Both types of insurance may require an appraisal or stated value for fine arts or antiques. I advise that you also obtain an appraisal for jewelry, china and crystal, antiques or any items of unusually high monetary value. Be selective in the jewelry that you plan to take overseas because it should be hand-carried. Jewelry, stocks, bonds and collections (such as stamps or coins) are typically excluded from insurance coverage in international move policies.

Overseas insurance policies will not extend to damage caused by "inherent vice" (the damage resulting from the specific relative nature of an item.). Today, most shipments are packed in steel containers where the temperatures for overseas cargo can vary to either extreme, and items that become damaged or spoiled such as wine, foods or furniture finishes will generally not be covered. Some shipping lines have refrigerated containers available, but these can adversely affect non-perishable items. To assure yourself of a good move and avoid confusion, clearly understand your corporate policy and the mover's policy. Do not leave anything to chance when you are moving your worldly possessions.

If you plan to take an automobile overseas, inquire about the country's insurance regulations. Some have mandatory "in country" insurance policies so be sure you are not paying twice for your coverage.

Packing tips:

- Let the movers pack breakable or valuable items so they are secure.
- Know the rules and liabilities for boxes packed by owner (referred to as "PBO"):

  Δ If you pack a box and it arrives dented and damaged, you can submit a claim for broken goods within that box.

  Δ If you pack a box and it arrives without obvious

damages or dents, any broken items in the box are your responsibility.

• Do not ship flammable or otherwise hazardous materials with your household goods. *M3*

Generally, you have 30 days to make a damages claim after a move, and it takes approximately 90 days to settle on the claim. Understand your employer's coverage and the moving company's rules and standard claim procedures, so that you can quickly resolve any problems.

Overseas

Be sure you will have the same comprehensive insurance overseas that you presently have. Inquire about how to file claims in the new country and in which currency you will be reimbursed, if loss or damage occurs. Insurance stipulations vary from country to country so know when and how your household goods and automobiles are affected. Inquire about policy changes for rates and differentials and check on mandatory liability health requirements. If you have a house in the U.S. that will be vacant or rented, be sure to note this status change with your insurance company.

In which country should you to stay in a large international hotel because it makes a better impression?

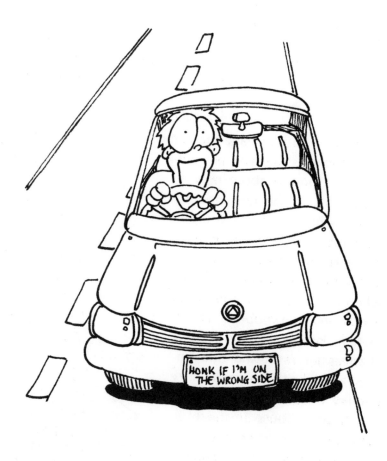

11

Settling In...Over There

Celebrate your arrival in the new country after all your hard work. Then, plan how you will adjust to the new country and commit yourselves to helping each other adapt and fully enjoy the coming experience.

As excited as you may be on arrival, euphoric feelings can quickly change to disillusionment when too many problems arise. This is especially true when you do not know how to solve the problem. At first, finding your way around an unknown subway system, using a strange telephone or becoming used to different terminology may seem adventuresome. As a little time passes and it hits home that you are really *living* in another country, instead of just *visiting*, you begin to feel the distance from family, friends and familiar and comforting experiences.

There is hope! The preparations you made prior to your arrival, plus the help of local relocation services, will help you settle in and feel at home sooner then you think. Relocation services provide information on education, shopping, household necessities, recreation, driving, legalities, medical and dental contacts plus many other assistance services.

Any company that has employees in foreign countries will have information about the above basics. Your company should pass these on to you prior to your departure so you can become familiar with them. This familiarity will further speed your establishment.

Check into tourist information bureaus upon your arrival. These bureaus typically have a wealth of information, some of which is free and will spur the family's excitement and anticipation. Be sure to pick up a map and study it *before* venturing out on the open road in a foreign country. European and Asian maps, road markings and signposts vary considerably from those in America.

A word of caution. No matter where you travel, in America or in other countries, there is always the possibility of a crime or robbery occurring. Unsuspecting tourists can be easy targets on night trains and busy tourist areas. Use the fanny paks you purchased before leaving the U.S. and be aware of your surroundings. Be especially careful of your passport and other forms of

identification. These are high theft items anywhere in the world. If you do have any problems, contact the American Embassy nearest you. See also the checklist for Travel Advisory in this book.

Regardless of how fast you settle in abroad, you will still be in a very different environment than the one you are used to and you *will* sense the difference. The inability to feel comfortable and at home in another country, as well as the emotional highs and lows that you can experience may make you feel as though you are losing some of your former self-confidence. These are passing phases of relocation, more noticeable when moving internationally. As people adapt and understand more of the local culture, they usually begin to enjoy the contrast. Families need to be sensitive to each other and share in their joys as well as frustrations. These efforts will ease the stress of cultural adjustments and bring you closer as a family as well.

Overseas relocations provide a wonderful opportunity for the entire family. Living in another country is one history lesson that will forever be imbedded in your minds and in your lives. Your goal is to fully enjoy all of it and make the most of every day and opportunity. In a few years it will end, and you will wonder where the time went and ask yourself "Am I ready to return home?" *M3*

Note: No matter how many cookbooks you now own, purchase one for the country in which you are living. It will simplify your dinner preparation tremendously. See *M3* for details.

In which country should you immediately present your business card and always wear a company lapel pin when conducting business?

"WHEN IN ROME ..."

12

Cultivating Overseas Business

Understanding the Climate

As I said earlier, international work associations are foremost a product of attitude, sealed with job expertise. *Before* you can make any gains in overseas business, you must first understand the culture and strategies of those with whom you are dealing. Find out where the emphasis lies in foreign business relationships and what is important to the people. If you must communicate in another language, you will most likely have an interpreter available; however, attempt to have a working knowledge of the language prior to arrival and try to learn the language of the country. This effort will be highly regarded.

Understand how they conduct business, their cultures and manners and *how they think.* Remember that while you are adjusting to the differences you experience, your new associates and co-workers will need to adjust to you as well. The Resources section of this handbook includes helpful books on cultures and manners under General International Information.

Thoroughly understand the authority you will have and

the title you will assume while overseas. What role will you have in day-to-day business negotiations? It is important that you are able to play an integral part in proposals or strategies so you can gain respect from the foreign managers with whom you will need to have continual contact.

Cultivate relationships in a manner that is appropriate for the culture in which you are conducting business. For example, in some countries, it is important to establish a more personal relationship, such as a social dinner, with your clients before you can arrange a business meeting. While in other countries, the social aspects are not as important; however, managers would never dream of beginning a business transaction without the standard "getting to know you chat." If you understand the manners, expectations and business practices of your associates, you will more successfully represent your company. Failure to learn the customs can result in lost business. Possibly one deal, possibly many deals—and *possibly* all deals!

There is still no substitute for "on the job training." No matter how much you read or hear about different countries and their work culture, you can still benefit by spending time with the manager you are succeeding. This time should be (preferably) at the work sight but if that is not possible, at least make a list of your questions and concerns and visit frequently with this manager. Continuity of work efforts and attitudes will help you and your corporation achieve the desired results.

As you work within various cultures, think of the people as being different, rather than better or worse than others. When working abroad, you must not only understand but strive to respect the varied conventions. I am

not implying that you attempt to change yourself or take on characteristics indicative of the country, simply appreciate the culture. The respect you show and your knowledge of procedures will greatly increase your chance of accomplishing business and personal goals.

Personal Business Strategies

The evaluation of the international assignment included learning exactly what your overseas responsibilities will be, as well as the nature of the assignment you will have when you return. Although the specifics of the return assignment have been greatly neglected in the past, more companies are becoming sensitive to this issue. Overseas positions for managers should be developmental positions and provide promotional opportunities.

Inquire about having a mentor to assist you in keeping current with home office practices (*Very* important!). If one is not suggested, select one or two people **yourself!**

Choose those on whom you *know* you can depend and who are also in a position to speak effectively on your behalf.

Ask these people to:

- Keep you informed of the home office activities, lingo and practices.
- Stay abreast of cultural changes in the office and community.
- Make your efforts and accomplishments known in the home office.
- Watch for opportunities for you.
- Throw your name in the hat when appropriate positions become available.
- Keep you informed of personnel changes, of who is doing what, etc.
- Periodically place news of you in the company newsletter.

Returning to the home office...

Do:

- Prepare yourself emotionally for changes. It's possible someone may have gotten, in your absence, the promotion you thought would be yours.
- Listen and be patient.
- Value colleagues' efforts.
- If you have not had a mentor, be sure management knows of your overseas' accomplishments.
- Contact Human Resources and obtain a position commitment.

Don't:

- Plunge in and make quick changes.
- Compare the overseas office to the home office.
- Constantly discuss how wonderful the overseas per-

sonnel were.
- Criticize your colleagues.

It can happen easily... Joe Brown working in London can become "that guy in the London office." **Help yourself!** To avoid returning to the home office as a stranger, plan occasional return trips to stay visible and active in home corporate activities and planning. Keep in touch with the people and with current business practices and procedures so that you feel at home when you walk in the door.

Brace yourself! Everyone who has gone through the process of repatriating, says it is *not easy*. However, if you can anticipate what to expect, think about the positives and give yourself time, you will soon feel comfortable in your former surroundings once again.

If your corporation has counseling services available, take advantage of them. Speaking about this challenging transition with an experienced and knowledgeable person will help you understand, but more importantly, validate your feelings. You'll come to know that these feelings are very *normal* and will eventually become a thing of the past.

In which country is it considered very rude to discuss business or hand out business cards at a social occasion?

"WHEN IN ROME ..."

13

Finances: Credit —What Credit?

Maintaining a sound credit record in your home country can be difficult while living overseas, especially if you are away for two years or more. Ironically, a college senior can receive an unsolicited credit card through the mail (even without a job), yet you will be surprised to find how quickly an established credit record can deteriorate without precautions. If you have never owned a house, or sold your house prior to departure, you may find it very difficult to obtain a mortgage when you return without taking the following precautions. Creditors and lenders look for established credit records on which to base their new loans. These basics are very simple to expedite and will help you avoid problems before they happen.

Before You Depart

- Establish an automatic deposit and payment system. This system is an easy method to routinely pay on accounts such as mortgage and active credit card accounts. (This avoids late payments which can lead to poor credit.)
- Arrange to have your paycheck automatically

deposited to avoid mail delays and banking hassels.
- Make a complete list of all your accounts and loans that require routine payments, noting the account number, address and telephone number.
- If you do not already have a savings account, establish one that you can easily add funds to while you are out of the country.
- Make arrangements for your investments. If you have a financial advisor, discuss your current and future investments. Establish methods to have these maintained while you are overseas.

While You Are Living Abroad

- Establish an account in a bank that offers you all the services you require and is able to assist you with (convenient) money transfers from country to country. Think about:
  Δ an automatic deposit system for the above mentioned items
  Δ their hours and convenience of locations
  Δ services, such as automatic teller machines
  Δ charges and dividends for checking and savings accounts
- Keep your home credit card active by using it at least once every six months, even if you acquire an overseas credit card.
- Maintain (and add to) savings and checking accounts in the U.S.
- Pay all accounts *on time* and *in full*.
- Keep a record of your credit transactions.
- Keep receipts for valuable overseas purchases., such as antiques. Keep abreast of the regulations that govern these purchases for returning to the U.S.

- Prior to leaving, request letters of recommendations from your overseas employer, bank manager and any other firms where you established credit while abroad.

Automobiles

If you purchase an automobile while living abroad, with the intent to bring it into the United States, know the customs regulations before you depart. Additional expense and delays can result if the vehicle does not conform to all U.S. safety and EPA requirements and guidelines at the time of its entry into the U.S.

Upon Your Return

- When applying for a major loan or mortgage, write to or visit the bank manager or vice president of a lending institution. If you speak to someone who does not have the authority to handle these matters, you can be turned down for credit.
- Take along overseas paid-in-full records with you when applying for (home) credit.
- Take along your letters of recommendation.
- Explain your unusual circumstances to the bank manager.
- When applying for new accounts, seek a small charge limit, and later request an increase.

In addition to these points, add whatever is relevant to your circumstances. These tips will help you avoid returning home with money in your pocket but *no credit* to your name.

In which country do the people take offense to foreigners crossing their arms?

AuPair/Homestay USA

During the time you were living abroad, perhaps you participated in a long-standing tradition, welcoming an au pair into your home to live as a family member, while caring for your children.

AuPair/Homestay USA allows you to continue that tradition. A program of World Learning, founded in 1932 as the U.S. Experiment in International Living, offers families a continuation of cross-cultural experience with a *one-year* child-care option. Their au pairs come from all areas of Western Europe, are between the ages of 18 and 25, English-speaking, fully screened and looking forward to living in the United States.

Once you are settled in your home, their network of more than 110 trained Community Co-ordinators throughout the U.S. offers support to both host family and au pair during your year together.

If you are interested in hosting an au pair in the United States, see Resources for complete details for AuPair/Homestay USA.

14

Repatriation

Managing the Cultural Changes of "Coming Home"

In the Wizard of Oz *Dorothy said
"There's no place like home, Auntie Em,
there's no place like home."*

That's what many people think when they *first* move abroad! They are sure they cannot survive without their favorite friends, snacks, clothes, pastimes, movies and television shows. I remember Americans who would venture miles and miles to find foods and items familiar to their homesick families. As time passes however, these items became less and less important, families settled in, began to feel quite comfortable and, later, found it rather enjoyable. The foods, pastimes, shows and clothes that once seemed vital to their existence had lost a bit of their luster. They even remarked that it was much easier to return to life abroad after their annual trip to America. In fact, they often felt eager to do so.

You will probably experience these common reactions after living abroad. Then all of a sudden, the news will come, just as it did when you moved overseas. Your life will be changing—once again. Only now you will be going "home." You will be returning to all those wonderful sights and sounds that you thought were ever so dear. But the trouble is you and your family will be different people after two, five or more years overseas. Not only in physical stature, from toddler to third grader or perhaps the moody eighth grader to high school junior, but you will also have grown due to your varied experiences.

Expatriates surmount the challenges of international employment and schooling and relish the joys of foreign travels and encounters. These facts make them unique among American friends. It is almost impossible for people to identify with an experience when they do not have the same frame of reference. Some of these friends have never traveled by airplane, let alone flown internationally. While living abroad, international flights are just another routine occurrence for expats. Not to mention the trips and travels for team competition, attending school with multicultural classmates, buying foreign-made clothes, spending Saturdays in London (or the nearest major city) and holidaying with their family on the continent.

 When children return to the states, they are especially excited to share their adventures and knowledge with their friends. The years spent abroad were *their lives* and they should be able to speak about them. However— they have to do so judiciously! Endless chatter about the *wonderful* overseas experiences will surely turn people off. Friends or acquaintances may view these references as making their town seem insignificant, unexciting and small by comparison. It would be the same situation as someone who had moved from any major city to a small town continually telling everyone how much better everything was in the big city. Encourage children to mix topics about Europe, Latin America or Asia with some to which everyone can relate.

Whether you spend your overseas assignment missing the familiar sights and sounds or absolutely immersing yourselves in the adventure, you will most probably still experience reentry shock. Even Dorothy might have had a few nostalgic moments when she returned to Kansas after all the glamour and excitement in Oz.

Even before you know you are moving back to the United States, try to stay abreast of America's fads and attire, TV shows, sayings, foods, and movies. These attempts will keep you current on life back home and when the time comes to move, will ease the transition. If your return is imminent, look into seminars for repatriates. For instance, the "Moving On" seminar by Focus Information Services in London. Consult Overseas Information Services in Resources.

One very good rule for the entire family to follow, especially as you are becoming reestablished at home, is to pay careful attention when others are speaking. You can learn a lot by listening during this transitional time. You can also ask whether your corporation has intercultural training available, and if some of you are still struggling with the adaptation after about six months, consider counseling assistance as well. As with the overseas adjustment, some members of your family will slip back into life in the U.S. easier than others. Companies that frequently send families abroad will have these services available to their employees and families who are repatriating, and if they do, take advantage of them.

The best advice I can offer is communicate and stay close to your family. It takes time, but you will adjust! Consider yourself richer for the experience and set about rediscovering America. Sometimes overseas assignments can give you a new perspective on an old situation—your own country! I would like to leave you with one final thought—a poem by Ida Scott Taylor.

One day at a time—this is enough.
Do not look back and grieve over the past,
for it is gone;
and do not be troubled about the future,
for it has not yet come!
Live in the present,
and make it so beautiful
that it will be worth remembering.

Flowers, arranged or potted, are common gifts in many countries. Do you know some of the customs which govern the following situations?

1. When are chrysanthemums used in arrangements in Europe?

2. In France, which flowers are only given to lovers?

3. How many flowers are considered an appropriate number to give to friends in most countries on the continent??

4. In Japan, what is considered an inappropriate gift for someone who is ill?

CHECKLISTS

BEFORE YOU FLY...

   We have had family members and visiting friends forget or lose airline tickets, misplace passports and travelers checks, (myself included). So we began using a pre-departure checklist, I hope it helps you as well. Check it *before* you leave for the airport.

- Valid passports. _____
- Visa, if required. _____
- Airline tickets. _____
- Hotel confirmation (address/telephone #). _____
- Travelers checks. _____
- Various denominations of foreign currency. _____
- Camera and calculator. _____
- Credit cards. _____
- Household inventory. _____
- Overseas moving company contact and telephone number. _____
- Furniture measurements so you can prepare a room plan before the moving personnel arrive. _____
- List of family medications and treatment. _____
- School transcripts and forms. _____
- Pertinent documentation (work permits). _____
- Address book with emergency (and other) telephone numbers. _____
- Contact numbers for setting up housekeeping in the new country. _____
- *Moving Minus Mishaps* and *"When in Rome..."* _____

Note: See also the checklists in M3 for additional details.

FINANCIAL ACCOUNTS

Safety deposit box number _____
   institution _____
   telephone number _____

Checking acct. number _____
   institution _____
   telephone number _____

Savings account number _____
   institution _____
   telephone number _____

Investments:	Company	Telephone #	Contact
stocks			
bonds			
real estate			
IRA			

Accountant _____
   company _____
   telephone _____

Credit Card number _____
   institution _____
   telephone number _____

Credit Card number _____
   institution _____
   telephone number _____

Others _____
_____
_____
_____

PERSONAL DOCUMENTS

Photocopy the appropriate items, store the originals in a safety deposit box and carry the copies with you.

	Date	Stored at:
Personal (updated) wills	_____	_____
Deeds	_____	_____
Marriage license	_____	_____
Birth certificates	_____	_____
Baptismal certificates	_____	_____
Confirmation certificates	_____	_____
Household inventory	_____	_____
House deed	_____	_____
Valuations/appraisals	_____	_____

List passport ID numbers

Name	Number
_____	_____
_____	_____
_____	_____

Automobiles
　registration number _____
　loan institution _____
　telephone number _____
Driver's license number _____

Insurance: Take claim forms and proof of your insurance with you. Inform your insurance agent of your new address and the date it will be effective. Create a list of your property, medical, personal and automobile policies. Include the telephone and policy numbers, address and contact person for each insurance. See also File for Pertinent Records Checklist in *M3*

FAMILY MEDICAL HISTORY

Make an up-to-date list for everyone in your family with the following information.

Person _____

  illness/accident _____

  treatment _____

  test results _____

  immunizations _____

  _____

  doctor _____

  hospital _____

  telephone _____

Before leaving the United States, develop a list with all of the following:

- Telephone access codes; physician and hospital telephone numbers.
- Directions to hospitals.
- Contacts for physicians who speak your own language.
- Procedures for routine, urgent and emergency care.

Take a bilingual dictionary, necessary insurance forms and card with the identification number. Know how your insurance coverage will be applied in the new country. ASAP upon arrival, visit the facility to confirm medical care procedures.

See *M3* for medical guidelines to survey new doctors, hospitals and medication information. Two checklists are included to provide you with domestic and international medication guidelines.

HOUSEHUNTING TRIP ABROAD

Be sure to read *Moving Minus Mishaps* before you embark on a househunting trip. The furniture and appliance measurement exercise will help you to estimate necessary overseas accommodations.

Carry with you:
  a camera _____
  tape measure _____
  furniture and appliance measurements _____
  pad and pencil _____
  calculator _____

Survey and measure the following:
  laundry facilities _____
  bedrooms _____
  sitting room _____
  kitchen _____
  living room _____
  bedrooms _____

During your househunting visit:
• Check the availability of parts and services for U.S. appliances you are considering moving abroad.
• *Critically* survey the room sizes, (many will be smaller and/or used for entirely different functions than those we are accustomed to in America.
• Take pictures of homes and rooms.

Note: If you move furniture abroad that you cannot use, it will have to be stored or returned at additional expense—and unnecessary wear and tear on your goods. Pack the appropriate owners manuals of all appliances.

TELEPHONE NUMBERS
AT A GLANCE

Check the Resources and Suggested Reading section for more information on these services. This separate listing is for your convenience.

Appliances Overseas Incorporated	(212) 545-8001
Centers for Disease Control immunization requirements	(404) 332-4559
Experiment in International Living	(202) 408-5380
Intercultural Press, Incorporated features books and videos on countries such as Japan, Hong Kong and Saudi Arabia	(207) 846-5168
International Association for Medical Assistance for Travelers	(716) 754-4883
International Driving Permit	1-800-972-2472
The International Nanny Association	(512) 454-6462
Overseas Citizens Services individual country information	(202) 647-3000 Dial ext. 1004 (on your fax machine)
State Department's Citizens Emergency Center. The Travelers System for political stability and many other services	(202) 647-5225

List additional telephone numbers:

_____ _____

_____ _____

_____ _____

TRAVEL ADVISORY

Plan your trip and travel route in advance and be sure everyone has a clear understanding of them. Keep a low profile, do not venture into unknown areas and *be alert.*

- Always carry your passport and an international driving permit if you have one.
- Let someone who is not going with you know your travel route and lodging plans.
- Make hotel reservations in advance.
- Avoid night trains when possible because vandals often travel on them. If you do use one, I suggest using a sleeping compartment.
- Keep to well-lighted and well-marked routes.
- Use a fanny pak instead of a purse and, if possible wear a baggy sweater over it.
- Be aware of local rules and always abide by them. Penalties for violations can be harsh in some countries.
- If you are traveling by car, have it serviced before leaving home. Lock valuable items in your trunk, carry a well-marked map and have these items with you:.
    - Δ insurance and registration cards
    - Δ first aid kit
    - Δ spare set of car keys
    - Δ flashlight and a whistle
    - Δ battery jumper cables
    - Δ flair and a white cloth for emergencies
    - Δ warm spare clothing and blankets.
      Stay safe and happy traveling!

APPLIANCES AND ELECTRONIC ITEMS

I am moving to England. Will my food processor and microwave work? What about my TV and VCR?

Appliances Overseas, international distributors of appliances and electronics for worldwide use, answers over 100,000 client's questions a month for families relocating overseas. In this section, Appliances Overseas answers some of the basic questions and provides the proper information regarding your appliances and electronic needs when moving overseas. They can also help you save 30-80% of your appliance/electronic costs.

There are three critical elements to electricity that are different in every country of the world: voltage, Hertz (cycles) and phase. For example, the U.S. is 115 V, 50 Hertz and one phase. Tokyo, Japan is 100 V, 50 Hertz and one and three phases. Certain appliances in your home are affected by all three of these elements, while other appliances are affected by only voltage.

BR Anchor Publishing has made special arrangements with the experts at Appliances Overseas to simplify this confusing issue for you. Mention this book and you will receive complimentary advice to fulfill your every appliance and electronic needs.

First of all, prepare a list on a room-by-room basis of all your current appliances and fax/mail this list to Appliances Overseas, (listed in Resources). They will review your list and professionally advise you about which of your appliances: (1) can be used "as is" with just a plug adapter, (2) can be used with the appropriate auto transformer or other device, or (3) should not be taken. In this case, you will need to secure a new unit in the correct electricity for your country.

Home entertainment is another important electronic issue. Televisions and video cassette recorders are special because in addition to the electricity, each country has a different broadcast system. There are over 30 different broadcast formats in use throughout the world, all incompatible with one another. If you want a system that will work and play tapes in the U.S. and every other country, you need a full multisystem TV and VCR.

It is important that you know that most appliances and electronic items cost 30, 50 and 80% more overseas than in the U.S. It is worth your while to learn about your appliance and electronic options (including sales and federal taxes, and all foreign duties, taxes and VATs,) while you are still in the United States.

Follow these five easy steps and you will be able to read your favorite book, prepare a meal and wash your clothes in the new country:
• Call, write or fax Appliances Overseas Incorporated.
• Send them your room-by-room appliance listing:
Example:
kitchen food processor   120 V, 50/60 HZ - 4.2A - 504W
• Give your specific foreign destination.
• Mention BR Anchor Publishing.
• Request an **Overseas Information Package**.

Upon receipt of your list, Appliances Overseas will advise you about what you need for the new country. They can either make your present appliances and electronic items work, or provide you with the new and appropriate items.

"WHEN IN ROME ..."

NOTES

Resources and Suggested Reading

ORGANIZATIONS ARE LISTED ALPHABETICALLY AND CATEGORICALLY

General International Information

◆ Appliances Overseas Incorporated, 276 Fifth Avenue, Suite 407, New York, NY 10001-4509. Telephone (212) 545-8001. FAX (212) 545-8005. See pages 82 and 83 for appliance information from Appliances Overseas.

◆ AuPair/Homestay USA, 1015 15th St., NW, Suite 750, Washington, DC 20005. (202) 408-5380. FAX (202) 408-5397. See page 70.

◆ Consumer Information Center-3C, R. Woods, PO Box 100, Pueblo, CO 81002 Send 50¢ for *Customs Tips for Travelers* #454Z, Information about duty, exemptions, prohibited items, pets and importing automobiles. Also, 50¢ for *Foreign Entry Requirements*, 456Z. Lists 200+ consulates, with details on visas and special requirements.

◆ *European Customs and Manners*, by Nancy L. Brananti and Elizabeth Devine. Pub. 1992, Meadowbrook Press. Tips on greetings, business and social customs, telephones, menus, money, transportation, legal matters and more! Check bookstores and libraries for updated books about Latin American and Asian Countries.

◆ IAMAT. International Association for Medical Assistance for Travelers, 417 Center St., Lewiston, NY 14092. Telephone (716) 754-4883. IAMAT has centers all over the world and can provide you with English- or French-speaking doctors, as well as other benefits. *M3*

◆ International Driving Permit. Request Form 1282 from: AAA Distribution Center, 13144 South Pulaski Road, Alsip, IL 60658. 1-800-972-2472. Cost $10.00. Requirements: To apply you must be 18 years old, have a valid U.S. state driving license and two passport size photos. You do not need to be an AAA member to obtain a permit.

Intercultural Training

◆ Bennett and Associates, Inc., 333 W. Wacker Drive, Suite 700, Chicago, IL 60606. Telephone (312) 444-2999. A consulting and training firm specializing in international human resources programs and support services. Their primary service areas include international assignment and (candidate) assessment programs, cross-cultural training, destination settling-in services and repatriation, global management development seminars and cross-cultural business-briefings.

◆ inlingua international, 230 South Broad St., 7th Floor Philadelphia, PA 19102. Telephone (215) 735-7646. With over 260 affiliates worldwide, inlingua provides customized language and intercultural training, as well as professional translation and interpreting services.Specialized consulting services help organizations to assess and resolve specific challenges such as cross-cultural team building, international joint-venture relations and technology transfer.

◆ Intercultural Press, Inc. PO. Box 700, Yarmouth, ME 04096. Features books and videos addressing intercultural challenges including Asian and Arabic countries. Telephone (207) 846-5168 for their latest catalog of publications.

◆ The Society for Intercultural Education, Training and Research (SIETAR) 808 17th Street, NW, Suite 200, Washington, DC 20006-3953. Telephone (202) 466-7883. The purpose of this professional organization, which has members in 60 nations, is to implement and promote cooperative interactions and effective communications among peoples of diverse cultures, races and ethnic groups. Write SIETAR for information about their programs, seminars, educational institutes and bi-monthly newsletter *Communique.*

Overseas Information Services

◆ *Background Notes.* Write Superintendent of Documents, U.S. Government Printing Office, Washington, DC 20402. Send $1.00 to receive a concise, authoritative pamphlet containing current information for any one of 170 countries.

◆ The Family Liaison Office, U.S. Department of State, Washington, DC 20520. Telephone (202) 647-1076. This office was created to respond to the needs of Foreign Service personnel and their family members. They provide assistance with education of dependent children, spouse/family member employment and crises management.

◆ FOCUS Information Services, Ltd., St. Mary Abbots Hall, Vicarage Gate, Kensington, London W8 4HN. Telephone 071-937-0050. A resource center for the international community in the UK providing information referrals, seminars and workshops on relocation-related topics, career support and personal skill development. Other support organizations:

Career Opportunities and Promotion for Expatriates
Van Diememstraat 202, 2518 VH, The Hague, The Netherlands
31-(0)70-392 40 03

Focus Career Services, Rue Lesbroussart 23, 1050, Bruxelles, Belgium. +32 264 665 30

WICE, 20, bd. du Montparnasse, 75015 Paris, France, 45 66 75 50

Focus International Career Services, 28 place de Brunes, CH 1257 Bardonnex, Geneva, Switzerland. +(022) 771 40 60.

◆ Japnaese Literature: (1) *Living In Tokyo*. This publication is usually presented to expatriates when they register in Tokyo. It is a versatile booklet that provides an ample overview of the city. (2) The Japanese Consulate. Write: Japan Information Center, 299 Park Avenue, 18th Floor, New York, NY 10171-0025 for comprehensive booklets and facts about Japan.

◆ Overseas Citizens Services, Dept. of State, Room. 4800, Washington, DC 20520 (for U.S. Consuls abroad). Dial (202) 647-3000, ext. 1004 *on your fax machine.* You will hear a recorded selection of available information for individual countries which can be sent to you via the fax machine. Assistance is available to Americans for passports, visas, medical and financial, income tax, emergencies, deaths, and disaster/evacuation problems.

◆ The Travelers Advisory System (U.S. Department of State). Telephone (202) 647-5225. Issues consular information sheets that provide the location and telephone number of the U.S. Embassy and Consulate in a country. They also have details about health, immigration regulations, currency exchange, the political stability of countries and known terrorist activities.

Assessment Services

◆ Moran, Stahl & Boyer International, 2555 55th St., Boulder, CO 80301. Telephone (303) 443-8440. Varied international services include a proprietary selection instrument called Overseas Assignment Inventory (OAI) which allows a company's human resource professionals to improve the expatriate selection process beyond assessing technical or job skills. The OAI helps identify the most cross-culturally adaptable individuals for assignments, appreciably lowering costly failure abroad. Moran, Stahl & Boyer International is a unit of Prudential Relocation Management, Valhalla, NY,

◆ Selection Research International, 7730 Carondelet Avenue, Suite. 412, St. Louis, MO 63105, Barry D. Kozloff, Pres. Telephone (314) 725-9269. SRI's core business since 1978 has been assisting organizations with the components of their international selection systems.

Their primary focus has been assessing employees and spouses for international assignment, identifying future international candidates and evaluating high potential and global managers.

International Schools

◆ *International Schools Services Directory*, by Peterson's, Inc., Dept. 15592, 202 Carnegie Center, Princeton, NJ 08543-2123 (USA). Telephone 1-800-338-3282 to order. Cost $34.95.

◆ *The World of Learning*, Europa Publications. Check Reference Sections in public or university libraries. Both of these publications are described in Chapter 6, Education: Points to Consider.

International Business and American Firms Abroad

◆ *Almanac of International Jobs and Careers*, by Ronald L. Krannich, Ph.D. and Caryl Rae Krannich, Ph.D, Impact Publications, Woodbridge, VA.

◆ The Conference Board, 845 Third Avenue, New York, NY 10022. Telephone (212) 339-0232. The Conference Board is one of the world's leading business membership organizations, connecting companies in more than 50 nations. Publications include *Across The Board* magazine, plus other periodicals, reports and studies analyzing and reporting on major business practices and evaluating global economic trends. In addition, The Board offers seminars and forums throughout the world.

◆ *The Directory of American Firms Operating in Foreign Countries*. World Trade Academy Press, 50 E. 42nd St., Ste. 509, New York, NY 10017. Three-volume, 2,500 page directory is invaluable for locating the more than 3,200 U.S. companies operating in over 120 countries. Includes employment statistics and contacts. $195.

◆ *Encyclopedia of Associations*, by Gale Research, Inc. Book Tower, Detroit, MI 48226. This essential four-volume reference work is updated annually. It is the single most authoritative resource for identifying nearly 22,000 national and international associations headquartered in the U.S. Can be purchased for $535.00.

◆ *Encyclopedia of Associations: International Organizations* by Gale Research, Inc. Detroit, MI. This two-volume reference identifies nearly 10,000 international associations headquartered abroad.

◆ *International Jobs, Where They Are—How to Get Them*, 1989, by Eric Kocher. A handbook for over 500 career opportunities around the world. Addison-Wesley Publishing Company, Inc

◆ National Foreign Trade Council, Inc., 1270 Avenue of the Americas, Suite 206, New York, NY 10020-1700. Telephone (212) 399-7128. This non-for-profit organization has more than 500 major firms whose primary goal is to enhance the international competitiveness of the U. S. private sector. Services include: realistic, widely-used overseas expatriate allowance data, human resource information for over 150 countries, seminars, manuals and international directories. **Note**: Visit the reference section of public or university libraries for these references and others for overseas companies and work opportunities, and graduate and professional schools.

Answers for the Flowers Quiz on page 74

In Europe:

Chrysanthemums are used only in funeral arrangements.

Red roses are only given to lovers.

Flowers are always given as a gift in uneven numbers with the exception of 13, which is considered to be bad luck.

In Japan:

Potted plants are never given to someone who is ill. A rooted plant has the connotation that you may be next in the ground.

Special Reports, by BR Anchor Publishing © 1993

Special Reports contain five pages of detailed information, packed with timely tips and professional resources. They were designed to supplement *Moving Minus Mishaps* with updated material, some of which would not be of interest to every reader. Whatever report topics are missing in this list compared to the one in *M3* are covered in *"When in Rome...."*

Written by Beverly D. Roman, author of *Moving Minus Mishaps* and *"When In Rome...."*

1. *Updated Supplement - More Relocation Savings*
   More cost saving information: the latest tips. Methods to save your money *and* your time.

2. *Evaluating a Move and Easing Relocation Trauma*
   How to evaluate relocation for one or two-income families, ease cultural changes, and reap the rewards of achieving a positive and successful relocation.

4. *Planning a Safe and Hassle-Free Relocation Trip*
   Ensuring safety on the road, during this difficult transition. Points for traveling in two cars, taking pets, making reservations, packing ready-to-eat snacks and more!

5. *Retirement Relocation—Estate Planning*
   Numerous considerations for retiring couples—from estate taxes to relocation decisions for your shifting priorities.

7. *Profitable Home Sales and Renovations*
   How to improve the value of homes and property through additions, renovations and attention to small details. Tips for profitable home sales.

9. *Preventing Medical Emergencies*
   Safeguard your family from accidents. Methods to avoid emergencies and safety hazards within your home.

11. *Real Estate Agents & Detailed Mortgage Information*
    How to choose a real estate agent, a buyer representative and survey lenders. Information on mortgage options and ways to eliminate househunting stress.

Special Reports, by BR Anchor Publishing © 1993

13. *Newlyweds, Dual-Career Marriages and—MOVING*
Assisting newlyweds with first home purchase, financial priorities, establishing and maintaining an excellent credit rating, and obtaining insurance coverage

15. *Buying And Renting Strategies for the 90s*
How to evaluate options. Renting is no longer considered a second cousin to buying a home; and it may even be more practical.

Special Reports by other authors:

14. *Successfully Relocating The Two-Career Couple*
By Joan M. Stevenson, owner of JOBNET, a career management firm in Allentown, Pennsylvania. How trailing spouses can successfully continue a career or create a new, exciting and fulfilling one in a new area.

18. *Assessing Relocation to Japan*
By Jacquie Raftery who lived in Tokyo, Japan, for five years. While there she worked for Tokyo Orientations, assisting expatriates with the cultural adjustments of the country. Comprehensive information to help you assess this move, and information for the everyday practicalities required.

Publication for young professionals
The Graduate's Handbook by Beverly D. Roman

This handbook contains professional resources, tips to move on a budget, plus it helps new grads to:
- prioritize their finances
- interview with confidence
- create an excellent credit history
- secure a safe residence
- look sharp with limited funds
- obtain comprehensive insurance
- avoid costly mistakes with household leases.

To order *The Graduate's Handbook* or Special Reports turn to the last page in this book.

Index

Customs and Manners Quiz
Answers

We Welcome Your
Comments and Suggestions

Send information to:
BR Anchor Publishing
P. O. Box 176
Hellertown, PA 18055-0176

Noted on page: _____

_____

_____

_____

_____

Source of my information:

_____

_____

Name _____

Street _____

City _____

State _____   ZIP _____ + _____
Company

_____

Telephone _____
YES, please add my name to your mailing list _____
☐ Newsletters
☐ Seminars
☐ Volume discounts
☐ Custom-designed books

ORDER FORM Satisfaction Guaranteed

Photocopy or return this page to: **BR ANCHOR PUBLISHING**
PO Box 176
Hellertown, PA 18055-0176

ORDERS 24 Hours a day Call toll-free 1-800-727-7691 OR—
FAX: (215) 865-4021 **INQUIRIES:** (215) 865-5331 8 a.m. to 5 p.m. ET

	PRICE	S/H
"When in Rome..." & Moving Minus Mishaps	$24.95	$3.00
Moving Minus Mishaps, Revised edition	$12.95	$2.00
The Graduate's Handbook	$10.00	$2.00

Special Reports $5.00 each, or 3/$13.00 postpaid
   One report ordered with a book, add $3.00 to order
Change-of-Address cards $2.50 postpaid
   One pack of cards ordered with a book, add $1.50 to order.

All orders shipped within 24 hours of receipt.

Please send order to:
Name _____
Address _____
City _____
State _____Zip _____Telephone _____
This is a gift ____Please sign card _____

"When in Rome..." and Moving Minus Mishaps _____
Moving Minus Mishaps____MMM & cards ___ MMM & SpecRpt ____
The Graduate's Handbook _____Change-of-Address cards _____
Special Reports #   ___ ___ ___ ___ ___ ___ ___ ___ ___

Order total	$	_____
PA address, 6% sales tax	$	_____
Shipping charges	$	_____
TOTAL	$	_____

Make checks payable to BR Anchor Publishing.

Thank you, we appreciate your order.

VISA ____MC _____#_____
Expiration date _____ Signature_____